Thank You,
MOON

Thank You,
MOON

Celebrating Nature's Nightlight

Melissa Stewart

illustrated by
Jessica Lanan

Alfred A. Knopf
New York

Thank you, Moon,
for being Earth's constant companion in space

Both Earth and the Moon have gravity—
a pulling force that tugs on objects. Earth's
strong gravity keeps the Moon orbiting in a
circle around us instead of flying off into space.

and making life on
our planet possible.

The Moon's gravity helps to keep Earth stable as it spins on its axis. Without that gentle tug, Earth would rock back and forth as it spins. Summers would be so scorching hot and winters so freezing cold that plants, animals, and other living things couldn't survive.

Thank you for guiding
tiny turtles to the sea

On a midsummer night, leatherback hatchlings break out of their eggs. They scramble to the surface of the sand and race toward the ocean. Bright moonlight reflecting off the water helps the little ones find their way to safety.

and dung beetles to their burrows.

When an African dung beetle smells poop, it scurries to the scene and sculpts the lumpy load into a giant ball. The Moon's glowing light helps the insect steer in a straight line as it rolls its mega-meal home.

Thank you for lighting the land,
so night monkeys can find their favorite fruits

Most monkeys are active during the day, but black-headed night monkeys wake up as the Sun goes down. On dark nights, they move cautiously through the trees. But when the Moon is bright, they can travel twice as far to find figs and other tasty fruits.

and nightjars can gorge on insects.

Each year, European nightjars migrate between their summer
home in Europe and their winter home in Africa. During the
Full Moon in late summer, they feed nonstop to fuel their flight.
Then, as the Moon wanes, the birds begin their long journey south.

Thank you, Moon, for giving lions
a chance to feed their families

On nights when just a sliver of Moon glows in the sky, a female lion crouches low in the grass and slowly slinks toward her prey. When the moment is right, she attacks. Then her mate and cubs join the feast.

and gazelles a chance to eat in peace.

On bright, moonlit nights, it's hard for lions to sneak up on prey. Instead of staying silent and still, Thomson's gazelles roam the savanna, grazing on grass.

Thank you for warning
zooplankton to dive deep

During chilly winters in the Arctic, the Sun never shines. The sky is dark all the time. When the Moon starts to rise, tiny zooplankton take action. They dive to the ocean's depths, so they can escape enemies that need light to hunt.

and kangaroo rats to stay hidden.

When the Moon is full, a Merriam's kangaroo rat doesn't leave its den. The dazzling glow lets the rodent know it will be an easy target for predators on the prowl.

Thank you for sending a signal
that triggers corals to spawn

A few nights after the Full Moon in midsummer, millions of stony corals release their eggs and sperm into the sea. Spawning at the same time increases the odds that plenty of coral larvae will form and grow into adults.

and joint pines to release their pollen.

When the Moon is full in July, sweet, sticky droplets full of pollen ooze out of a joint pine's colorful cones. The liquid sparkles in the moonlight, attracting hungry flies and moths. And as the insects feed, they spread pollen from plant to plant, so new seeds can form.

But most of all, thank you, Moon,
for enchanting us with your ever-changing beauty,
night after night,

The biggest, brightest Moons are called Supermoons.
They occur when the Full Moon is at its closest point to Earth.

and, sometimes, surprising us in the daytime, too.

We usually think of the Sun lighting up our days and the Moon glowing at night. But for part of each month, you may be able to see the Moon during the day—if you look closely.

More About the Moon

Lighting Up the Night

Our Moon is the biggest, brightest object in the night sky.
But it doesn't produce the light we see—the Sun does.

As sunlight strikes the Moon's surface, some of the light bounces
back into space. When that reflected light reaches our eyes,
the Moon seems to glow.

Phases of the Moon

The Moon orbits in a circle around Earth approximately once a month.

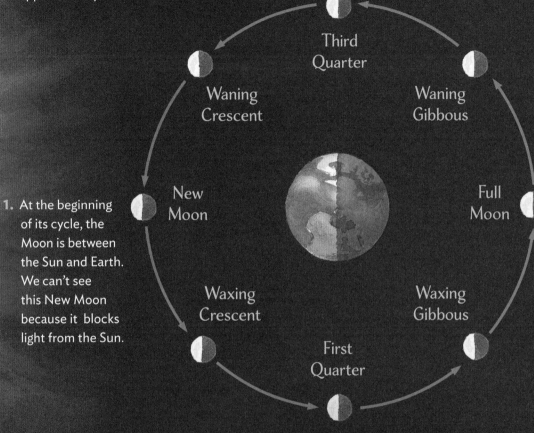

Third Quarter

Waning Crescent

Waning Gibbous

New Moon

Full Moon

1. At the beginning of its cycle, the Moon is between the Sun and Earth. We can't see this New Moon because it blocks light from the Sun.

3. After about two weeks, we see a Full Moon. Then we see less and less of the Moon each night—until its next cycle.

Waxing Crescent

Waxing Gibbous

First Quarter

2. As the Moon continues to orbit, it blocks less and less sunlight each night, and we see more and more of the Moon.

The Moon's phases as seen from Earth:

| New Moon | Waxing Crescent | First Quarter | Waxing Gibbous | Full Moon | Waning Gibbous | Third Quarter | Waning Crescent |

More About Creatures that Depend on the Moon

Leatherback sea turtle

Scientific Name: *Dermochelys coriacea*

Size: 6 to 7 feet (1.8 to 2.1 m) long

Habitat: Ocean

Range: Worldwide

Diet: Sea jellies

Predators: Crabs, lizards, raccoons, coyotes, birds, large fish, squid, octopus

Lifespan: 50 to 100 years

Field Note: An adult leatherback sea turtle weighs about as much as a cow.

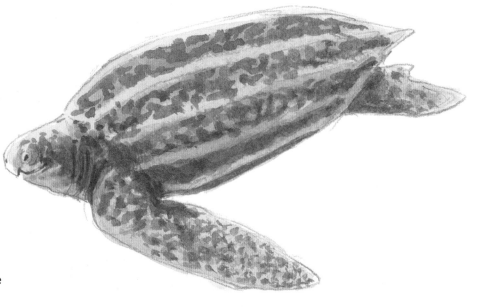

Dung beetle

Scientific Name: *Scarabaeus zambesianus*

Size: 1 inch (2.5 cm) long

Habitat: Grasslands

Range: East Africa

Diet: Dung

Predators: Bats, birds, lizards, foxes

Lifespan: 3 to 5 years

Field Note: More than 6,000 species of dung beetles live on Earth. Some feed on cow patties and deer droppings in North America.

Black-headed night monkey

Scientific Name: *Aotus nigriceps*

Size: 14 inches (36 cm) long

Habitat: Rain forests

Range: Brazil, Bolivia, Peru

Diet: Mostly fruit, some flowers, leaves, and insects

Predators: Owls, snakes, wild cats

Lifespan: Up to 20 years

Field Note: Why are black-headed night monkeys active at night? So they can avoid predators and eat in peace while other monkeys sleep.

European nightjar

Scientific Name: *Caprimulgus europaeus*

Size: 9 to 11 inches (24 to 28 cm) long

Habitat: Grasslands, open woodlands

Range: Africa, Eurasia

Diet: Insects

Predators: Foxes, martens, hedgehogs, weasels, hawks, falcons, snakes

Lifespan: Up to 12 years

Field Note: Male nightjars attract females with a churring call that contains up to 1,900 notes a minute.

Lion

Scientific Name: *Panthera leo*

Size: 8 to 10 feet (2.4 to 3 m)

Habitat: Grasslands

Range: Central and southern Africa

Diet: Gazelle, impala, wildebeest, zebras

Predators: Humans

Lifespan: 10 to 15 years

Field Note: Lions can run 50 miles (80 km) per hour and jump up to 36 feet (11 m).

Thomson's gazelle

Scientific Name: *Eudorcas thomsonii*

Size: 31 to 47 inches (80 to 120 cm) long

Habitat: Grasslands

Range: Kenya, Tanzania

Diet: Grasses, shrubs

Predators: Lions, cheetahs, leopards, hyenas

Lifespan: 10 to 15 years

Field Note: Some people call Thomson's gazelles "tommies" for short.

Zooplankton

Scientific Name: Various

Size: Microscopic

Habitat: Oceans

Range: Worldwide

Diet: Algae

Predators: Fish, whales, crabs, shrimp, and many other ocean animals

Lifespan: Varies

Field Note: The term "zooplankton" describes a wide range of microscopic animals and the eggs and larvae of larger animals that drift with the currents.

Merriam's kangaroo rat

Scientific Name: *Dipodomys merriami*

Size: 14 inches (36 cm) long

Habitat: Deserts

Range: Southwestern United States, Mexico

Diet: Seeds

Predators: Owls, coyotes, foxes, bobcats, snakes

Lifespan: 9 years

Field Note: This little rodent has a long tail and large back feet. It usually hops or jumps instead of running.

Stony coral

Scientific Name: *Acropora millepora*

Size: 0.04 to 0.08 inches (1 to 2 mm) wide

Habitat: Coral reefs

Range: Indo-Pacific oceans

Diet: Plankton, bacteria

Predators: Sea stars

Lifespan: Unknown

Field Note: This coral comes in a rainbow of colors, including pink, purple, red, yellowish green, bright green, or orangey gold.

Joint pine

Scientific Name: *Ephedra foeminea*

Size: 6 feet (1.8 m) tall

Habitat: Rocky hills

Range: Mediterranean region

Diet: Make their own food

Predators: Insects

Lifespan: Unknown

Field Note: This shrub, which is used to make a medicine for asthma, is the only plant scientists know of that depends on moonlight to complete its life cycle.

Selected Sources

Daly, Martin, Philip R. Behrends, Margo I. Wilson, and Lucia F. Jacobs. "Behavioural Modulation of Predation Risk: Moonlight Avoidance and Crepuscular Compensation in a Nocturnal Desert Rodent, *Dipodomys merriami.*" *Animal Behaviour.* 1992: 44(1), pp. 1–9.

Kronfeld-Schor, Noga, Davide Dominoni, Horacio de la Iglesia, Oren Levy, Erik D. Herzog, Tamar Dayan, and Charlotte Helfrich-Forster. "Chronobiology by Moonlight." *Proceedings of the Royal Society B.* August 22, 2013. royalsocietypublishing.org/doi/10.1098/rspb.2012.3088

Lang, Kristina Cawthon. "Primate Factsheets: Owl Monkey (Aotus) Taxonomy, Morphology & Ecology." *Primate Info Net.* Madison, WI: Wisconsin National Primate Research Center Library, University of Wisconsin–Madison, July 18, 2005. primate.wisc.edu/primate-info-net/pin-factsheets /pin-factsheet-owl-monkey/

Last, Kim S., Laura Hobbs, Jørgen Berge, Andrew S. Brierley, and Finlo Cottier. "Moonlight Drives Ocean-Scale Mass Vertical Migration of Zooplankton During the Arctic Winter." *Current Biology.* 26, January 2016, pp. 244–251.

Norevik, Gabriel, Susanne Åkesson, Arne Andersson, Johan Bäckman, and Anders Hedenström. "The Lunar Cycle Drives Migration of a Nocturnal Bird." *PLOS Biology.* October 15, 2019. doi.org/10.1371/journal.pbio.3000456

Palmer, Meredith S., John Fieberg, Alexandra Swanson, Margaret Kosmala, and Craig Packer. "A 'Dynamic' Landscape of Fear: Prey Responses to Spatiotemporal Variations in Predation Risk Across the Lunar Cycle." *Ecology Letters.* 20(11), November 2017, pp. 1364–1373.

Shultz, David. "Plant Releases Its Pollen in the Full Moon." *Science.* April 1, 2015. sciencemag.org/news/2015/04/plant-releases-its-pollen-full-moon

Stewart. Melissa. Personal observations recorded in nature and travel journals, 1989–present.

University of Michigan Museum of Zoology Animal Diversity Web: animaldiversity.org

Wayman, Erin. "Moonlight Shapes How Some Animals Move, Grow, and Even Sing." *Science News.* July 8, 2019. sciencenews.org/article /moon-animals-light-behavior-lunar-phases

Witherington, Blair E., R. Erik Martin, and Robbin N. Trindell. *Understanding, Assessing, and Resolving Light-Pollution Problems on Sea Turtle Nesting Beaches.* St. Petersburg, FL: Florida Fish and Wildlife Conservation Commission, 2014.

Further Reading

Krautwurst, Terry. *Night Science for Kids: Exploring the World After Dark.* Asheville, NC: Lark Books, 2003.

McNulty, Stacy. *Moon! Earth's Best Friend.* New York: Holt, 2019.

Salas, Laura Purdie. *If You Were the Moon.* Minneapolis, MN: Millbrook Press, 2017.

Singer, Marilyn. *A Full Moon Is Rising.* New York: Lee & Low Books, 2016.

Solar System Exploration: Earth's Moon: solarsystem.nasa.gov/moons/earths-moon/overview

Thank you, Katherine, for suggesting that I write this book
and skillfully shepherding it to publication.
—M.S.

To Rose, who never gave up on me
—J.L.

Text copyright © 2023 by Melissa Stewart
Jacket art and interior illustrations copyright © 2023 by Jessica Lanan

Visit us on the Web! rhcbooks.com

Educators and librarians, for a variety of teaching tools, visit us at RHTeachersLibrarians.com

Library of Congress Cataloging-in-Publication Data
Names: Stewart, Melissa, author. | Lanan, Jessica, illustrator. Title: Thank you, moon / Melissa Stewart, Jessica Lanan.
Description: First edition. | New York : Alfred A. Knopf, [2023] | Includes bibliographical references. | Audience: Ages 3–7 |
Summary: "Animals adapt their behavior to the different phases of the moon."—Provided by publisher.
Identifiers: LCCN 2022022159 (print) | LCCN 2022022160 (ebook) | ISBN 978-0-593-43507-6 (hardcover) |
ISBN 978-0-593-43508-3 (lib. bdg.) | ISBN 978-0-593-43509-0 (ebook)
Subjects: LCSH: Nocturnal animals—Adaptation—Juvenile literature. | Moon—Phases—Juvenile literature. |
Animal behavior—Juvenile literature. | Plants—Effect of the moon on—Juvenile literature.
Classification: LCC QL755.5 .S893 2023 (print) | LCC QL755.5 (ebook) | DDC 591.5/18—dc23/eng/20220630

The text of this book is set in 17-point Elaina Semi Serif and 11.25-point Ideal Sans.
The illustrations were created with watercolor and water-soluble colored pencil.
Book design by Taline Boghosian

MANUFACTURED IN CHINA   10 9 8 7 6 5 4 3 2 1   First Edition